Minimum Wage Maximum Results

Finding, hiring, training & bringing out the best in your employees

by

Robert K. McIntosh

This publication is designed to provide accurate and authoritative information in regard to the subject matter covered. It is sold with the understanding that the author is not engaged in rendering legal, accounting, or other professional service. If legal advice or other expert advice is required, the services of a competent professional person should be sought.

© 1997 Robert K. McIntosh
All rights reserved
Printed in the United States of America

   Orem, Utah 84058

This publication may not be reproduced, stored in a retrieval system, or transmitted in whole or in part, in any form or by any means, electronic, mechanical, photocopying, recording, or otherwise, without the prior written permission of the author.

Minimum Wage, Maximum Results

Table of Contents

Introduction 2

Chapter 1 - The Good News and The Bad News 5

Chapter 2 - Minimum Wage, Maximum Worth 13

Chapter 3 - Why Do They Do What They Do 17

Chapter 4 - A Game Plan for Developing Employees 25

Chapter 5 - Finding and Hiring 31

Chapter 6 - Setting Employee Expectations 43

Chapter 7 - Training That Makes A Difference! 55

Chapter 8 - Positive Reinforcement 63

Chapter 9 - Drill Sergeant, Buddy Buddy, Coach 69

Chapter 10- You Get What You Reward 77

Chapter 11-Turning Problem Employees Around 106

Chapter 12- Safety and Security 117

Conclusion 125

Acknowledgements

Any book is the result of the efforts of many people. I express my sincere appreciation to the following:

To my wife, Susan, for her support and encouragement with my business successes and failures. To our children, Rob, David, Michelle, Deborah, and Nathan who have worked in and managed many of our businesses.

To our sons and daughters in law, Lonnie, Greg, Ramona and Bronwyn, who have also supported our business ventures.

To Lee Benson, John Linn, John Lovern, and Harvey Turner for their friendship, encouragement, and suggestions.

To Nancy Gardner for her work with the manuscript.

To Jim Reed for designing the book cover.

To Colby Olds, Robert Evelyn, and Eli Escamilla for their work in seeing the book from manuscript to printing.

And finally, to my father, Robert V. McIntosh who taught me the meaning and importance of a good work ethic.

Chapter One

The Good News and The Bad News

Owning and managing a business is one of the most satisfying experiences I have ever undertaken, while at the same time easily the most challenging. In fact, my dream of being my own boss has sometimes turned into a nightmare. Someone wrote the following about the challenges of business ownership:

"If you are working for a boss who makes you put in 8 hours a day with only Saturday and Sunday off, and only 2 weeks sick leave; and if you have to pay 25 percent of your income as taxes; and worrying about your own problems lets you sleep only 8 to 10 hours a night - don't fret about it."

Just work and save and soon you can own your own business and be the boss. You can then work 14 hours a day, 7 days a week with no vacation, and you can't afford to get sick. Seventy-five percent of your income will go for taxes, and you'll be lucky if worrying about your own and all your employees' problems lets you get 2 hours sleep at night. So, work hard and save your money and someday you can be the boss.

Being "the boss" carries with it many responsibilities. These can be divided into two managerial categories - managing facilities and managing people. Which of these is the most difficult? That's right, managing people. The human factor is the most unpredictable in a business venture and it is usually the one that is not taken into consideration when evaluating a business opportunity. The people we hire can literally make or break our business. This is certainly true with minimum wage employees as well.

My experience with entry level workers over the past thirty years has taught me many things. An important lesson I have learned can be illustrated when I hired one of my sons to manage a business. He had been managing the store for about one month when I stopped in to see how he was doing. The moment I walked into the store I could tell there was something wrong. Tension was in the air.

He walked up to me and in an exasperated voice said, "Dad, I need to talk with you right now!"

We walked out the back door into the parking lot and I said, "What's wrong?"

He replied. "It's these employees! I can't stand it! How many times do I need to remind them to do something?"

I knew then I had forgotten to tell him an important thing about entry level workers.

I said. "When you leave the store at the end of the day what are you thinking about?"

He said. "I'm thinking about the business!"

"When our employees leave what are they thinking about?"

He thought a moment and said. "Most of them are thinking, 'Party time!'"

I replied. "Right, and why are you thinking about the business?"

He replied. "Because I care."

At that moment I could see the light go on above his head and he said to me, "You mean some of our employees don't care?"

I said. "That's exactly right. No one cares about our business as much as we do!"

That is the challenge all business owners and managers face. No one cares as much as we do. That is a frightening thought! We entrust our business, a huge investment, to people who don't care as much as we do. Our challenge is to motivate our employees to care about our customers and our business while we are paying them to do so!

Here are five challenges we might face when hiring minimum wage employees:
1. Most are young, between the ages of 16 and 25. Because of this, many have priorities that are more

important than their job. Therefore, they often do not put their job first.
2. Most have had little experience with customer service and therefore lack the background essential in any business that deals with the public.
3. Some bring negative attitudes about working which reflects on their ability to relate well with others and respond well to customers.
4. Many have not yet learned what it means to have a good work ethic. A common attitude with some young people is to do just enough to get by.
5. Many are part-time employees who are not making a career out of working for us. Therefore, we must help them see why doing a good job for us will benefit them in the future.

Sound formidable? It is, and there is another problem. Most of us were not born managers. The doctor certainly didn't exclaim to my parents at my birth, "It's a manager!"

The ability to manage people is learned. Granted, some people seem to have been born with certain skills that help them relate positively with people. But the ability to get people to do what you want them to do because they want to do it is the essence of leadership -- and those skills can be learned.

That's the bad news. Here's the good news. First, we don't have to learn everything by experience.

The Good News and The Bad News

A young executive heard that the Chairman of the Board was retiring so he set up a meeting to talk with him.

The first thing he asked was, "Sir, I really want to succeed with this company. What can I do to be successful?" The elderly gentleman leaned back in his chair and said, "Johnson, just two words, 'Right decisions!'"

The young man replied, "But sir, how do I make right decisions?"

"Johnson, just one word, 'Experience!'"

"But sir how do I gain experience?"

"Just two words, Johnson, 'Bad decisions!'"

You don't have to make all the bad decisions to gain experience. However, you can learn from people like me who have already made plenty of bad decisions. You can also talk with other business owners and ask them what mistakes they've made.

And there is some more good news! Because minimum wage employees are, for the most part, young, they are trainable. I have often said to people, "Give me a seventeen or eighteen year old who hasn't worked for anyone, and if they are trainable I'll turn them into a responsible employee."

And finally, more good news! Minimum wage employees need money. And they usually need it desperately for such things as car payments, insurance, and school expenses.

My experience the past thirty years has shown me that most minimum wage employees are trainable. The key is the way we treat them and our ability to train them properly.

In the chapters that follow, I'll share with you what I have learned about motivating minimum wage employees.

Key Points in Chapter One

1. Those who care the most about a business are the owners and managers.

2. Most employees, if trained and treated properly, will choose to do their best at work.

3. The skills necessary to effectively manage people can be learned.

Chapter Two

Minimum Wage, Maximum Worth

Although our employees are entry level, minimum wage earners, they are all we have and they are of great worth to us. They should be regarded accordingly. Contrast this outlook with a business owner I met in the East. When I shared the idea that we need to value our employees, he replied, "I disagree with you. You don't know the type of people we hire here. We hire from the bottom of the barrel!"

When he said that, my mind pictured what is usually at the bottom of a barrel. No wonder this owner had problems with his business!

There is a concept that has helped me realize how important our employees are. It is called "The last five feet of the pipeline." There are activities that go on up the pipeline that our customers don't see and probably don't care about. Such things as

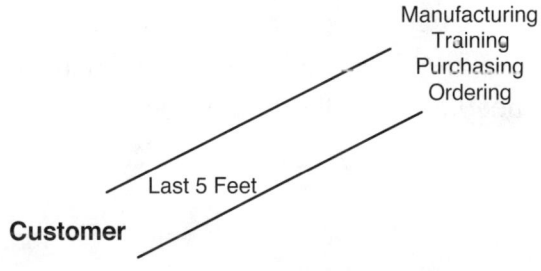

manufacturing of our products, meetings that we hold to prepare advertising campaigns, employee training, and ordering of products, to name a few. What the customer cares about is the delivery of the product or service - what takes place in the "last five feet of the pipeline." Let me share an example. When I travel to present seminars, I usually fly. As an airline passenger, who in United Airlines is in the "last five feet of the pipeline"? Right! The flight attendants are in the last five feet. I am not concerned about who manufactured the airplane, how much it cost or even who the pilot is! The flight attendants represent the entire pipe line. From my point of view they are United Airlines.

Suppose as I get on the airplane I stumble and the flight attendant responds by saying in an angry voice, "Sir, could you please hurry, there's a line behind you!"

What will I be thinking as I walk down the aisle of the airplane? Probably something like this -"This is the most unfriendly airline I have ever flown on!" What did I just do? I judged the entire airline company, every pilot, flight attendant, and employee by one person.

Now, in your business, who is in the last five feet? Possibly a minimum wage employee. Should a customer have a bad experience with this employee, what will the customer do? He will judge your entire business by that one employee. If you own a franchise it's even worse! He will judge your entire franchise.

So, how valuable are your employees? They may be minimum wage but we need to consider them to be of maximum worth.

Key Points in Chapter two

1. Customers judge an entire business by the employee who interacts with them.

2. Our employees are, therefore, the key to either making, or breaking a business.

Chapter 3

Why Do They Do What They Do?

Most managers of entry level workers have at one time or another exclaimed, "Why do they do what they do?" Some may ask that question every day!

Making the effort to understand our employees can pay big dividends in the long run. Here's why! If we can understand their individual needs we discover what I call their "hot button." That which will motivate them to do what we want them to do.

One lesson I have learned over the years is that what is motivational to one employee may not necessarily be the same for another. One manager I know couldn't figure out why his teen-age employees weren't excited about a sales contest that had as its reward free tickets to the symphony!

Senator Robert F. Bennett in his excellent book *Gaining Control* states that all behavior can be traced back to an individual's needs and wants. In other words, we do what we do to satisfy a need or want. He identifies four needs that are universal to all people. These four needs are parts of a wheel and when all of them (needs) are met, our lives can move forward smoothly.

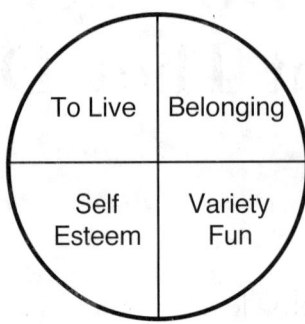

When one of these basic needs is not being met, the wheel goes flat. When this happens people focus all of their energy on that need even to the point of ignoring other needs.

Let's examine each of these needs and how they affect the behavior of minimum wage employees.

The Need to Live

All people are going to die. Yet most young people do not think about death as a reality. They have the idea they will never die. Most adults try and take care of their physical body through proper eating and safety. They also seek a quality of life that provides comfort and security. For the adult employee, food and shelter are major drives to earn a wage. However, for the young entry level worker, these basic needs are often being met by their parents and many will neglect their physical safety to meet one of the other three needs.

The Need for Love/Belonging

Because most minimum wage employees are young their peer group is the #1 influence in their life. They will miss work to be with their friends, they will give product away to impress friends, and they will risk health and safety to be part of the group.

We can use this as a powerful motivator if we can build a feeling of teamwork among our employees. I have had some employees become best friends and reinforce each other to do their best on the job. There is, of course, a down side to this if they reinforce each other in negative ways. Young people have told me that one of the most positive aspects of their job is the people they work with.

The Need for Self-Esteem

How we feel about ourselves determines how we behave. A negative attitude is usually the result of a negative self image.

Our entry level workers are at an age where their self-esteem is very fragile. Many young people I have worked with have a low self image. This is perhaps a result of the society we live in where so much is negative. With the traditional family in jeopardy, many young people have been raised in negative home environments. Young people today seem to be shouting, "Hey, notice me!"

Managers and supervisors who are sensitive to this need can use it as a powerful motivator. Sharing what we expect with new employees, helping them acquire the necessary job skills and noticing the good things they do can help to build their self esteem. One person put it this way, "When people feel good about themselves, they produce better results."

The Need for Variety

How many times have you heard young people say, "It's boring!" when referring to a school class or job. Our employees want variety. That's why they are constantly doing things - movies, parties, hobbies, vacations. They lose interest quickly. Therefore, if we can make their work environment fun and interesting they will respond better.

An occasional crew party is something they can look forward to and can be motivational. Joking around, having a sense of humor while working makes their job more enjoyable. Humor in the workplace is like the oil in an automobile engine: it reduces the friction.

In 1995, I conducted a survey, with the help of a local college marketing class, of over 300 minimum wage employees. They ranged in age from 16 to 23. Our goal was to find out what motivated them. The results were somewhat surprising. I had read in most management books that money was not the most important thing to most workers. This survey showed me that for entry level workers this was absolutely not true. Money is the most motivating factor for them. Money far outweighed praise for a job well done or time off with pay. Although these are important factors in job satisfaction, money was the major motivating factor because they need to satisfy immediate needs.

After the survey it became clear to me why this was so. Look again at the four basic needs and how money is common to each of them. (In Chapter 10 we will examine specific ways to use money as a reward.)

1. The Need for Life
   Money provides the basic things young people want - a car, dates and clothing.
2. The Need for Belonging
   Money gives them the ability to do things with their friends.
3. The Need for Self-Esteem
   Money is an indicator to them of their worth. A raise or a bonus means a lot.
4. The Need for Variety
   Money provides them the opportunity to do fun and different things.

One of our challenges is to find out why our employees want their job and what they will do with the money they earn. Their answer to these questions is their hot button. The answer will be different for each employee. But, whatever their needs, if we can find out what they are, and consciously work toward helping to fulfill that need, we can begin to establish with them an "importance" to their job that otherwise might be lacking. By doing this we establish a link between their needs and their job.

I developed a form entitled, "Employee Motivation Survey" that I give to each new employee I hire. This helps me discover what motivates them. Then, by pushing their "hot button" I can motivate them to be their best while working for me.

Employee Motivation Survey

Rank in order from 1 to 8 the following factors according to what is important to you with 1 being the most important, 2 the next, etc.

_____ Raise in pay
_____ Pleasant working environment
_____ Praise and recognition for doing a good job
_____ Interesting and challenging work
_____ Friendliness of people I work with
_____ Clear understanding of what is expected of me
_____ Fairness of my manager
_____ Cash bonus

To help us meet your needs as one of our team members, please answer the following questions:

1. Do you like to be complimented or praised in front of other employees?

Yes   No

2. Do you mind being corrected in front of other employees?

Yes   No

3. Does competition motivate you?

Yes   No

4.   Should someone compliment or praise you, which of the following people would mean the most to you. Rank in order of first, second, etc.

_____ Other team members
_____ Customers
_____ Owner
_____ Manager

5.   Which of the following rewards for a job well done would you prefer? Rank in order of first, second, etc.

_____ Verbal praise
_____ Money
_____ Prize such as a CD, etc.

Rank which prize you would rather receive. Rank in order of first, second, etc.

   _____ CD
   _____ Movie ticket
   _____ Gift certificate for clothing
   _____ Gift certificate for lunch/dinner
   _____ Time off with pay
   _____ Ticket for a free car wash
   _____ (anything else)_____

Key Points in Chapter Three

1. We need to make an effort to understand what motivates our employees-their "hot button."

2. What is motivational to one employee may not be motivational to another.

Chapter Four

A Game Plan for Developing Employees

Over the past thirty years, I have hired and trained over five hundred minimum wage workers. One of the important lessons I have learned is this: we must invest time and effort if we want them to behave responsibly and give good customer service.

I shall never forget the very first employee I hired. I was 23 and had just opened our first business, a fast food restaurant. For some reason, I assumed that when I hired someone they would automatically behave like I wanted them to. After two weeks, I was very upset with this employee and sat down with her and pointed out what I perceived to be the problems with her performance. She replied, "I didn't know you expected me to do that! Had I known that's what you wanted I would have done it."

To say the least, I was embarrassed at my neglect. That experience and many others taught me that I needed a game plan to help me develop and train my employees. Things just don't magically happen! It's like someone has said, "There are three kinds of people: those who watch things happen; those who make things happen; and those who wonder what happened." I determined I wanted to be the type of owner and manager who made things happen.

For this reason, at a young age I began developing a game plan to develop my employees. Over the years I have added to it and refined it. This game plan consisted of five steps for working with my entry level employees. Each step is important in this process. A small investment of time with our employees can pay big dividends later on.

Here are the five steps:

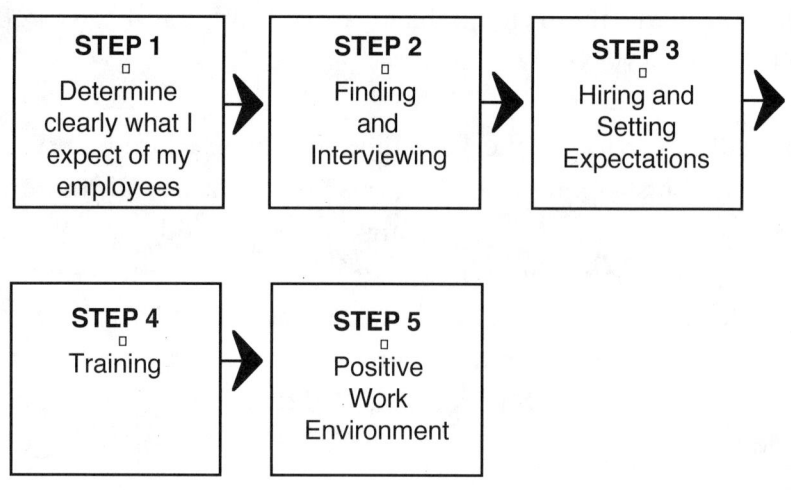

Step 1 - <u>My Expectations</u>
We might refer to this as our vision of the ideal employee.

This vision clarifies our expectations or what we want our employees to do. Steven R. Covey in his book, *The Seven Habits of Highly Effective People,* gives as one of his habits, "Begin with the end in mind". This first step is the key to all other steps in the model for it requires us to determine what kind of behavior we want our employees to demonstrate. Take out a blank sheet of paper and make a list of what you want your employees to be like. This exercise will become something like a mission statement for your team. When I did this, my list contained such qualities as: friendly with customers, dependable, skilled at the job, and a team player.

Now, with the end in mind, let's look at steps 2, 3, 4 and 5 of the above model to see how to go about realizing our goal:

Step 2 - <u>Finding and Interviewing</u>
Some business owners have told me that their greatest challenge is finding people to interview. Others have said their biggest problem is weeding through all the applications they receive. This is a critical step because without people to interview there is no use worrying about training.

Step 3 - <u>Hiring and setting expectations</u>
When we set expectations we clearly outline to a new employee how we want them to perform. In other words, we help employees "catch a vision" of what we expect of them. Setting expectations begins from the moment we start looking for employees and continues through the hiring and training of the employee.

Step 4 - <u>Training</u>
Once our expectations are in the mind of our employees, training is the process that gives them the tools to be able to do what we want them to do.

There are two critical steps in this phase: First, determine what skills your employees need to be successful in their job, and second, develop systems that will help them be successful.

Step 5 - <u>Positive Work Environment</u>
A positive work environment creates an atmosphere wherein our employees choose to do what they know we expect of them. Such things as positive feedback and incentives help to create a desire within our employees to do their job well. It is the very essence of employee motivation.

Having studied human behavior both at university and in my own businesses, I have personally witnessed the powerful effect of a positive work environment.

Let's now look at each step in my game plan to develop employees.

Key points in Chapter Four

1. Those who manage employees are in the business of "developing people."

2. Developing employees requires an investment of time and effort.

3. It also requires a "game plan" as to what we will do to develop our people.

Chapter Five

Finding and Interviewing

She was tall, blue-eyed and very pretty. Instantly I thought, "I don't need to interview her. She'll make a great employee." How wrong I was! She cost me a lot of money because of her know-it-all attitude and poor work ethic. I found out later that she really didn't need a job as her parents were supporting her. All she wanted was to have money to play around.

Since that time, I have been much more careful with my hiring procedures! One of my business associates, Bill Byrne, taught me a great lesson. He said "Bob, when you work with minimum wage employees you are in the ATR business. Attracting, Training, and Retaining good people." So, let's talk about attracting good employees.

The people we hire determine the way our customers are treated. I have found that most business owners spend too little time determining who they will hire. As owners we are faced with so many pressures that hiring properly can become a low priority. I have been told by some owners that anyone who can cloud up a mirror is good enough for them! The problem with that attitude is we will pay for it later, just like I did with my blue-eyed employee! So will our customers!

One of my managers gave me the ideal solution for hiring. He said to me, "I know how to increase customer service in our store! All we have to do is hire people who love people!" When he said that I remembered some statistics I had read:

- 5% of all people walking the streets of America are pathological criminals, they just have not been caught!
- 85% are nice people
- 10% are wonderful people

My experience has been, and I shared this with my manager, that the same statistics apply to the people we interview for a job.

- 5% hate people
- 85% are not quite sure how they feel about life and people
- 10% love people

The problem with my manager's suggestion is there are not enough people who love people. In fact, if we have one employee who loves people we are lucky and we had better hold on to him/her.

Here is the challenge: most of the people we deal with are among the 85% who are not sure. Because we hire people who have not made up their mind about life, we have to help them choose to be responsible employees! This process begins from the moment we start looking for potential employees. By the way, I try to avoid the 5% who hate people!

Finding Potential Employees

The lower the unemployment rate the more difficult it is to find people to hire. Those who hire entry level and minimum wage workers will find it increasingly more difficult as we approach the year 2000 and beyond. The reason being that there has been a decline in the birthrate for the past number of years and there just will not be enough young people to go around! Therefore, the competition to get and keep these workers will increase. A business owner must be constantly looking for potential customer friendly employees. Here are some suggestions I have found helpful.

1. The single most effective way to find new employees is through existing employees. Some of my finest employees have been found in this manner. Some business owners I know give an incentive to their employees for referring someone to them. They give a bonus of $25 or $50 dollars if the referral is hired. I always remind my employees that we are looking for employees who are people oriented.

2. Keep a file on potential employees. We have people come in to our store from time to time looking for a job. Whether we are hiring or not I have them fill out an application. These applications are kept in a file for future reference when we are hiring.

3. Post a "Now Hiring Friendly People" sign. Current customers are valuable in two ways: First, they may be looking for work themselves and, second, they may tell someone else that we are hiring. I have known some business owners who printed up a one page flyer explaining the details of the job. These

are placed by the "Now Hiring" sign so that customers can take a reminder with them about the position.

4. Establish relationships with local high school and college business programs. Get to know business teachers and explain to them that you are always on the look out for friendly, and outgoing young people. Sometimes these teachers will refer students to you. We have hired a number of employees from our local schools.

5. Let local churches and synagogues know you are hiring friendly people. Some of my best employees have come through this avenue.

6. Use of temporary agencies. Temporary agencies can be a good source for potential employees. When using a temporary agency let them know the type of people you want to employ.

7. Look for customer friendly people as you frequent other businesses. Hand them your business card and say, "Should you ever need another job please give me a call".

8. Advertise in the newspaper. Some owners have told me this has been very successful for them. I suppose it depends on the area as this method has been a time waster for me. Every employee I have hired from a newspaper ad has turned out to be a "dud"!

9. Youth agencies. Many towns and cities have local youth organizations such as the Boys and Girls Club. These can be

a resource for potential employees.

10. Correction departments. Some business owners have hired young people who were in a correction facility. They have indicated that they were always to work on time because they were delivered by the correction officers. Sometimes these youth are in a correction facility for minor violations. I haven't tried this one yet!

The Selection Process

Once you have people interested in working for you, it is extremely important that you develop employee selection criteria. I'm not suggesting something that will take hours with each applicant. I am suggesting that we need to feel comfortable with the people we hire. I've been through the thinking process, "Well, I'll put my new employees on a two-week trial basis and, if things don't work out, I'll just let them go." That kind of thinking just doesn't work! It costs time and money to train new employees. What is needed is a little more time up front in the selection process.

So far as I have experienced it, there are only four reasons the people we hire do not work out.

1. We hire the wrong person for the job.
2. We do not train them well.
3. We treat them in a negative manner.
4. The employee is totally irresponsible.

Did you notice that three of the four are, to a great degree, within our control? Let's look at the first one, hiring the wrong person. Later in this book, we'll discuss training and how we treat our employees.

I follow two steps that help me determine the type of employee I am looking for. First, I develop a description of what the requirements are for the particular position I need to fill. Second, I make a list of the skills an employee needs to fulfill this position description. Let me give you an example. Suppose I need to hire an employee to work at the front counter of my fast food restaurant.

Position Description
   Necessary Skills
1. Wait on customers.
     a. The ability to communicate well with people.

2. Make sandwiches.
     b. Good head-hand coordination and the ability to follow directions and work fast.

3. Use the cash register.
     c. The ability to count change and work the cash register properly.

4. Work with other employees.
     d. The ability to get along well with others.

5. Answer the telephone.
     e. Ability to use the telephone in a professional manner.

For every position in your business you need a position

description and an idea of the skills that an employee will need to be successful.

Getting the Know the Applicant
Once you have in mind what the employee will do and what skills are needed, you are prepared to screen applicants. How do you find out if they are the right person for the job? I have heard many managers say, "I go by gut feeling." My experience has been that gut feeling is often wrong. We must have a system that will help us get to know the people we are hiring. Here are some tools that can help us avoid the costly mistake of hiring the wrong person.

1. Conduct a background check on the applicant. This can be done through checking their credit rating or their driving record.

2. Have the applicant take a pre-employment aptitude and/or honesty profile. These profiles will tell you if the applicant has the ability to do the job you want and, given the opportunity, would the employee steal from you. Many companies produce these profiles at a nominal fee ($7-$10). To find a listing of these companies, search on the Internet under "Employee theft, employee honesty or employee aptitude."

3. Check references. This is extremely important. I usually call at least two references. The type of questions you ask will determine what you learn about the applicant. Here are the questions I ask:
   a. "What were the dates of the applicant's employment with you?"

b. "Did the applicant fulfill the job requirements to your satisfaction?"
c. "How did the applicant relate with management?"
d. "What types of problems did the applicant have with coworkers?"
e. "If given the opportunity, would you hire the applicant again?"

Conducting an Effective Interview

This is one of the most challenging aspects of the hiring process. Interviewing effectively is a skill that can be learned. Some managers I know consider an effective interview to be a three or four minute talk where they explain to the applicant the virtues of their business and then say, "How does that sound to you?" Anybody with an IQ over fifty would say, "That sounds just fine." An effective interview has two purposes. First, it helps us get to know the applicant. When I interview, I am looking for three things:

1. Ability. Do they have the ability to do the job?

2. Attitude. Do they have a positive, outgoing and teachable attitude?

3. Compatibility. Will they fit in with my existing team?
And second, an effective interview begins setting the expectations of the applicant as to what I require.

Here are some ideas about the actual interview.

1. Conduct the interview in a place where you will not be

interrupted by the telephone or other people. An initial interview takes ten to fifteen minutes of total concentration.

2. Use an employment application form. This form should contain key information such as their local address; past employment experience and history; hobbies and activities they have been involved in; references; and their days and hours of availability to work.

3. Develop interview questions that are open-ended and will help you get to know the applicant. An open-ended question is one that cannot be answered "yes" or "no." These questions require the applicant to say something. Here is where listening skills are essential. A good interviewer will listen with their eyes as much as their ears. Watch the applicant's eyes and body language as they respond. Listen carefully to their responses. If the response is not clear, say "Would you please repeat that?" Here are some open-ended questions I use.

Interview Questions

"My job for the next few minutes is to get to know you well enough to make a judgment as to whether I should hire you."

A. Past employment history. Review employment application with applicant.
1. What specifically did you do at your last job?
2. What did you like most about your last job?
3. Like least?
4. When I call your last supervisor, what will he/she tell me are your best qualities?
5. What will he/she tell me are your two greatest weaknesses?

B. Interest level in the position
   6. Why are you seeking employment? (What will they use their money for!)
   7. Based on what you know, describe your level of interest in working for us.
   8. How long will you be able to work for us?

C. Getting to know the applicant
   9. What do you know about our company?
   10. If you were in my place what would you look for in a potential employee?
   11. What are your goals in life?
   12. What hobbies do you have?
   13. What type of behavior would you consider dishonest in this type of job?

D. Ability
   14. This job requires certain skills. (Describe the skills required) Why do you
       think you would be able to be successful at this job?
   15. What situations in your life might cause you to have a problem getting to work on time or fulfilling the job requirements?

Effective interviewing is a skill we can learn. It means talking less and listening more. When all is said and done, we are responsible for the people we hire. A little time invested up front can yield much later on.

Key Points in Chapter Five

1. We are in the "ATR" business: attracting, training, and retaining good employees.

2. Attracting good employees must be a major priority of owners and managers.

3. We need a position description and an idea of the skills required for each position in our business.

4. We need to spend some quality time interviewing and selecting the people we hire.

Chapter Six

Setting Employee Expectations

What is wrong with the following situation?

John was hired to work in a fast food restaurant. This was his first experience working with fast food. His last job was as a stock boy in a grocery store. Stock boys do not usually go out of their way to help customers. They have a job to do, stock shelves, and they do it.

When John was hired to work in the restaurant, his manager made no mention of how customers were to be treated. So, John was shocked when his first month's evaluation read, "Needs to be friendlier with customers".

Who was at fault here, John or his manager?

Because his manager did not let him know exactly how customers were to be treated, John went by what was expected at his last job.

Expectations are powerful motivators. An expectation is what we as owners and managers expect our employees to do.

However, if we do not share these expectations, employees will use past experience or their own current ideas as to how a job is to be done.

Most young people come to their job with little understanding as to what is expected of them. When we establish clear expectations up front we help to form their mind-set to their job.

We have two opportunities to influence employee behavior:

- Before the behavior occurs

- After the behavior occurs

Setting employee expectations is what we do <u>before</u> the behavior occurs. Here is a powerful principle I have learned: Employees are more open to direction and guidance at the moment of hiring than they are three months after we have hired them. Why is this true? At the moment of hiring the new employee wants to please us and impress us. The job is new and exciting so the employee is psychologically open to direction. Three months later the employee thinks he/she knows everything!

Therefore, you as an owner or manager have a golden opportunity at the time of hiring to set the new employees expectations and direction.

Here are two tools I have used to accomplish this.
1. An employee understanding of expectations form.
This is a type of employment agreement yet does not carry

legal ramifications. That's why I call it an "understanding," not an "agreement".

To be effective, the understanding of expectations must be simple - one page. The simpler the better. A marriage license is usually one page, a divorce decree hundreds!

When I created my own employee understanding form I sat down and made a list of the expectations I had of my employees. These expectations came from Step 1 of my model, "What I expect of my employees". They divided nicely into three areas: Customer service, team work, responsibility.

When I hire a new employee I go over this with them sentence by sentence. I introduce it something like this. "Janice, I want you to have a successful experience here. To assist you I have made a list of what I expect as your employer. Let's go over it sentence by sentence. You will see that I am going to ask you to sign it indicating you have read it and you understand clearly what is expected of you. Should you have any questions or concerns please bring them up to me."

We then go through the understanding of expectations together. This usually takes about 5 to 10 minutes. I have found 5 minutes up front with an employee can save hours of problems later on.

After we have gone through our discussion I give the employee two copies to sign. One goes in their employee file and the other they keep (see an example of this form at the end of this chapter).

2. Team rules and disciplinary policy.
I have had many business owners tell me that had they used a form like this it would have saved them countless headaches with employees. This is possibly one of the most helpful ideas I have ever discovered. A team rules and disciplinary policy accomplishes at least two things!

1. It sets in the employee's mind up-front exactly what they should and should not do.

I have a friend who travels the country giving seminars on employee theft. He told me that he would probably be out of a job if employers would tell their employees up-front what the rules of honesty are for their business and then develop a way to check to insure they are honest.

2. It lets the employee know exactly what will happen if they violate the rules. (An example of what I use is also found at the end of this chapter.)

You will note that I have two sections: Grounds for immediate termination and serious violations.

I spell out to my employees what they can expect should they violate these team rules.

Again, I review this with them and have them sign two copies.

Should a problem occur later, I can go to the employee's file and take out the signed sheet and review it with them.

I always tell new employees that I can become their very best friend or their worst enemy. Some day they will need a recommendation for another job. If they do a good job for me, I'll be a valuable reference. If they do a poor job, they had better not use me as a reference. I also give them a form, "What Employers Look For in Good Employees." I have them review this to reinforce what they can learn from being a responsible employee for me.

Setting employee expectations up-front is a powerful way to begin developing the behavior of your employees.

How do you present these two forms to existing employees? To help them buy into it, I would give them the two forms and ask them for their input and suggestions. In this way they feel a part of the process.

Employee Understanding of Expectations

WHAT YOU CAN EXPECT FROM US
We realize that you will probably not make a career out of working with us. However, your employment with us can be of great help to your future. If you will do your part, we can promise you that you will learn the following skills:

1. Customer Service — How to effectively deal with customers
2. Teamwork — How to work effectively with a team of employees
3. Leadership — How to take the initiative at a job and become a leader
4. Discipline — How to develop self control which is critical to success in life

Each of these skills will help you grow and develop, thus preparing yourself for a secure future. We will provide the opportunities, but it is up to you.

WHAT WE EXPECT FROM YOU

Customer Service
You agree to provide excellent customer service so that our customers:

1. Feel welcome when they first enter our store
2. Feel that we care about them as individuals.
3. Feel that we appreciate their business.
4. Feel that we care about the quality of their product.
5. Feel that we care when they have a complaint.

Teamwork
You agree to be a team player so that other team members:
1. Can count on you.
2. Can trust you.
3. Enjoy working with you.

Responsibility
You agree to be a responsible employee so that your owner and manager:
1. Can trust you.
2. Feel you care about the store and your job.

You understand that true service is helping customers feel good about themselves. You fully understand what your owner/manager expects of you.

Employee Signature_____ Date_____

Manager Signature_____ Date_____

First Evaluation _____ Date Goal_____

Team Rules and Disciplinary Policy

PURPOSE: Our business will be as successful as the team we have hired. You are an important member of our team. For our team to be successful we need rules to guide what we do. These rules will help you work with other team members and will let you know up front what we expect of you. Violations of team rules affect everyone. This policy will explain team rules and the results you can expect when a rule is broken.

TEAM RULE VIOLATIONS.

There are two types:
1. **Grounds for immediate termination**
   - Stealing or mishandling of money
   - Using drugs or alcohol while working
   - Giving away products or merchandise
   - Refusing to follow a direct order from the manager or supervisor
   - Assault of a team member or customer
   - Being rude to customers

2. **Serious Violations**
    Failing to:
    Greet, talk with, and thank our customers
    Answer the telephone in a friendly manner
    Suggest other products to our customers
    Handle customer complaints in a friendly, sensitive manner
    Stay busy at all times so that other employees do not have to do your work
    Get along with other team members - no backbiting, gossiping, putting down

Setting Employee Expectations

      Failing to be to work on time every shift
      Bringing friends into the work area
      Receiving or making personal calls except in an emergency
      Failing to follow approved opening and closing procedures
      Failing to keep the workplace clean

Should one of these team rules be violated, the following steps will happen until the behavior is either corrected or the employee terminated:

      First - You will be reminded as to the proper behavior.
      Second - You will have a sit-down, face-to-face talk with your manager.
      Third - You will sign a written warning form which will be placed in your file.
      Fourth - Your work hours will be reduced.
      Fifth - You will be terminated.

I have read "Team Rules and Disciplinary Policy" and understand the rules and what will happen should I violate the rules.

Employee _____ Date _____

What Employers Look For In Good Employees

What kind of employee are you?

Statements from companies that hire many people:

1. First of all, honesty and reliability are certainly two fundamental virtues which all employers look for. No matter how bright or promising in other respects a young person might be, he will be passed up if he cannot be depended upon.
   The Perfect Circle Co.

2. Naturally such fundamental qualifications as honesty and fine physical condition are essential. We want the ability to take criticism and take it graciously. We need people who can get along well with others. Nothing so interrupts an organization as does a troublemaker, an alibier, or a worker with a "chip on his shoulder".
   The Proctor and Gamble Co.

3. We look for leadership qualities as well as intelligence. A person's scholastic standing is important, but even though he ranked at the head of his class, if he could not get along well with others he probably would not get along well with us.
   National Broadcasting Co., Inc.

4. The basic requirements that we seek to discover -- in addition to the fundamental characteristics of honesty, industry, and loyalty --
   1. Is he or she prompt?
   2. Does he understand instructions and retain them?

Setting Employee Expectations

   3. Is he accurate and dependable?
   4. Does he require constant supervision?
   5. Does he set a good example in conduct, appearance, and attitude?
   6. Does he recognize what is beyond his scope?
   7. Does he refrain from assuming too much authority?

Westinghouse Electric & Manufacturing Co.

5. The qualities they have developed or failed to develop in school will weigh heavily for or against them - not just when getting a job but toward getting ahead, too.

   BE ORDERLY
   DEVELOP EMOTIONAL STABILITY
   COOPERATE WITH OTHERS
   ACCEPT CORRECTION IN THE RIGHT SPIRIT
   ANTICIPATE THE NEEDS OF THE JOB AHEAD
   DEVELOP SELF-DISCIPLINE
   BE PROMPT
   AVOID THE CURSE OF THE EVER-READY ALIBI
   BE POLITE

Mrs. E.E. Brooke Inc., Personal Service
(She found jobs for 40,000 people)

6. Employees for the most part are dismissed or fired from their jobs for a few reasons: <u>disloyalty, dishonesty, lack of cooperation, repulsive personality, lack of inclination to work, utter disregard for rules, talking negatively about fellow workers, laziness, and being a drinker or using illegal drugs.</u>

Professor L.R. Humphreys, Utah State University

Key Points in Chapter Six

1. Employees are more open to direction at the moment of hiring than they are a few months after we have hired them.

2. One way to set the direction of a new employee is to use a form entitled "Employee Understanding of expectations." and a form entitled "Team Rules and Disciplinary Policy."

3. A little time spent up front can save hours later on.

Chapter Seven

Training That Makes a Difference

What you believe about training will, to a great degree, determine how your employees treat your customers. While most managers I have talked with agree that proper training of their employees is important, very few do much in the area of customer service. Many managers train their employees in the operational duties but neglect customer service. Two excuses are frequently given for this:

I do not have time, and I do not know how to train.

Let us examine each of these excuses.
First - *I do not have time.* When you stop to think about it, you really do not have time to not train your employees. Consider the results of poor training:

- Poor Customer Service
- Low Employee Morale
- Poor Product Delivery
- Loss of Sales
- Loss of Income

I have an axiom that sums up why training is so important. "Training the front line increases the bottom line!"

 Why don't employees learn what we teach them?
 1. We are not clear as to what we want them to do.
 2. We do not involve them in the learning experience.
 3. We do not ask for feedback

Proper training of employees does not have to take a lot of time. Sometimes people tend to think of training as putting new employees through a two day seminar. Most people only remember 10% what they hear the first time.

Therefore, short training sessions extended over a longer period of time where the employee is able to practice the skills learned is a more manageable method.

Second - *I do not know how to train.*

You need not be a professional teacher or trainer to train your employees. Training employees involves four simple steps:

 1. Tell them how you want it done
 2. Show them how to do it
 3. Involve them in doing it
 4. Give them feedback

These four steps have been used successfully by many companies.

Here are a few suggestions that can help you implement these four steps.
1. Develop an operations manual with sections for each

particular aspect of your business. Topics might include:
- Customer Service
- Safety
- Opening Procedures
- Product Preparation

In the manual you will tell your employees exactly how you want things done. This is what many established franchises cite as one of the biggest keys to their success. They give their franchisees a proven system.

2. Assign one of your best employees as a trainer for new employees. This employee can show the new employee how you want things done. For example, how to greet customers and handle customer questions. The trainer can also watch the new employee and give feedback.

3. The owner/manager must be a model of excellent customer service. If you are going to "talk the talk" you must be willing to "walk the walk." The best customer service person in the business needs to be the owner or manager!

4. Develop systems or checklists for everything you want your employees to do.

One of the areas I want my employees to be good at from the very start is customer service. I am very concerned about turning over my customers to a poorly trained employee.

To accomplish this I developed a customer service quick start program for my employees. This program is based on two ideas.

First, once I hire an employee, they know I want our customers treated exceptionally well. However, they might not understand what "exceptionally well" means. Therefore, I need to make it very clear how they are to treat our customers. The more specific we are the better! When we deal in generalities people rarely do what we want.

Second, the key to training is to give people systems. Systems are checklists employees can follow to accomplish something. I believe that the systems we have in place are as valuable as the people we hire.

How many times do people fail at a job because they are not given the tools to do it! I have had employees quit and I have let them go when it was not their fault, it was mine!

My Customer Service Quick Start Program gives my employees a specific system as to how to treat the customer.

The first thing I do is identify the different phases of an employee - customer experience. In my business I identified four different phases. These might be compared to a baseball diamond. To hit a home run the employee must touch all four bases with our customers.

>First base- the greeting
>Second base- talking with our customers
>Third base- suggestive selling
>Home plate- proper handling of the money and thanking the customer

Once these four areas were identified I developed a checklist for each one and put them on a laminated card. The four cards plus one for answering the telephone are at the end of the chapter.

At the time I hire a new employee he/she is given the Customer Service Quick Start Program and asked to learn what is on each card. Some employees will pick it up quickly and others will need time.

You can develop checklists for every important area of your business. To begin, simply ask yourself, "What skills do my employees need to be able to fulfill my job expectations?" Then develop a checklist for each of these skills. Again, a checklist is a step-by-step road map as to exactly how you want things done.

Remember, training the front line increases the bottom line!

GREETING THE CUSTOMER
Customer Service Quick Start #1

PURPOSE: To make our customers feel welcome

BENEFIT TO YOU: You will develop the ability to make people feel comfortable.

☞ Always smile!!

☞ Greet each customer within 10 seconds — look up, be aware of when customers come in

☞ Look at the customer — good eye contact

☞ Say: "Hi. Welcome to _____."
"Hi. What can I get for you?"
"Hi. I'll be right with you."

REMEMBER, YOU MAY NOT GET A SECOND CHANCE TO MAKE A GOOD FIRST IMPRESSION!

TALKING WITH THE CUSTOMER
Customer Service Quick Start #2

PURPOSE: To make our customers feel we care

BENEFIT TO YOU: You will develop the ability to communicate well with people.

SUBJECT	WHAT TO SAY
Weather	"Is it still warm (cold) out there today?"
School	"How are your classes going?"
Business	"Taking a break from the office?"
Noticing something positive about our customers	"Your children are sure cute."
	"I really like your perfume."
	"Your shirt is great."
Suggesting other products	"Are you aware of our other products?"
	"What size drink would you like?"
	"We have a great selection of chips."
	"How about a fresh cookie?"

REMEMBER: PEOPLE DON'T CARE HOW MUCH YOU KNOW UNTIL THEY KNOW HOW MUCH YOU CARE!

THANKING OUR CUSTOMERS
Customer Service Quick Start #3

PURPOSE: To leave the customer with a good feeling about our business

BENEFIT TO YOU: You will develop the attitude of appreciation which is essential to a happy life.

☞ Look at the customer

☞ Smile

☞ Say to the customer:
  - *"Have a great day!"*   *"Have a great weekend."*
  - *"I hope you enjoy that sandwich."*   *"Good luck on your exam."*
  - *"Let me know how you like that sandwich."*

☞ Give the change to the customer as follows:
  1. Put large bills on top of the cash drawer before putting them in the drawer.
  2. Count the change out loud to the customer.
  3. Put the money in the customer's hand.

REMEMBER: THE LAST THING A CUSTOMER REMEMBERS IS WHAT YOU SAY OR DO AS THEY ARE LEAVING OUR RESTAURANT

Training That Makes a Difference

PROPER USE OF THE TELEPHONE
Customer Service Quick Start #4

PURPOSE: To encourage customers to come in to our restaurant

BENEFIT TO YOU: You will learn to use the telephone in a profesional manner.

☞ Smile — People can tell if you are happy!

☞ Say: "Good afternoon _____ . This is _____."

☞ Answering commonly asked questions:

QUESTION	ANSWER
"How late are you open?"	"We are open until ___ and I can have a sandwich ready for you."
"I'd like to place an order."	"Sure. What can I get for you?"
"Do you have any specials today?"	"Yes, our special is _____."

☞ End the telephone call with: "Thank you for calling."

REMEMBER: NEVER LEAVE A CUSTOMER ON HOLD FOR MORE THAN 30 SECONDS. IF YOU ARE BUSY, TAKE THEIR NUMBER AND CALL THEM BACK.

ANSWERING UPSET CUSTOMERS
Customer Service Quick Start #5

PURPOSE: To keep customers coming back to our restaurant

BENEFIT TO YOU: You will learn how to deal with difficult situations.

☞ When a customer has a complaint, do the following:
1. Listen carefully so you understand the customer's concern
2. Say: "I'm sorry that happened."
3. Solve the problem using the following guidelines:

CUSTOMER COMPLAINT	WHAT TO SAY TO THE CUSTOMER
"I can't believe I had to wait so long!"	"I'm sorry. Can I get you a free drink?"
"You put too much mayo on."	"I'm sorry. Can I fix you another sandwich?"
"Your prices are pretty high."	"Our sandwiches are very high quality. Some places may charge less, but we pride ourselves on making your sandwich the way you want it."

REMEMBER: CUSTOMERS MAY NOT ALWAYS BE RIGHT, BUT THEY ARE THE CUSTOMER! AND, AN UPSET CUSTOMER TREATED RIGHT CAN BECOME OUR MOST LOYAL CUSTOMER!

Key Points in Chapter Seven

1. Everything that happens in a business is dependent on one thing-training!

2. Short training sessions over a period of time are more effective than one long training session.

3. One of the most important keys to effective training is to give new employees systems or check lists for each thing we want them to do.

4. Assign a model employee as a trainer for new employees.

5. Owners and managers teach more by what they "do" than by what they "say."

Chapter Eight

Positive Work Environment

A bright capable young woman explained to me one day how much she disliked her job and why she was going to quit as soon as possible. Very curious, I asked her why she felt this way. She explained that she really enjoyed what she was doing but the problem was her boss. He was very negative and insensitive to the feelings of his employees. He was referred to around the office as "the intimidator!" When he left to go on business trips, his employees were ecstatic and hoped he never returned. I could multiply this young woman's experience hundreds and hundreds of times. Many managers are totally unaware of how they come across to their employees and many do not understand how to create an atmosphere where employees feel motivated to do their best.

One of the greatest concerns in business management over the past 50 years has been how managers can influence the behavior of their employees. Over the years management fads have come and gone. The problem for most business managers who work with minimum wage employees is that they have had little or no training in human relations skills. Therefore, turnover is a constant problem. A supervisor of entry level workers must be a psychologist, a baby sitter, a warden and a mediator to handle the myriad of challenges in the workplace today. There are relatively few books written to help the thousands of managers who work with minimum wage employees.

Too often, by the time we have learned through experience how to deal with our employees, we have lost our business. Benjamin Franklin said it well, "Experience keeps a dear school and fools will learn in no other".

Possibly one of the greatest lessons I have learned managing entry level workers is that people frequently do not do what I tell them to do. Herein has been my greatest challenge, "How do I get my employees to treat my customers in a positive manner?" "How do I get them to be responsible?" "How do I keep good employees?"

Aubrey Daniels in his book *Bringing Out the Best in People*, says, "People do what they do because of what happens to them when they do it."

Through his studies of people he has found that consequences have a profound influence on the way people behave and how they feel about their job.

The consequence he has found that most influences productive behavior is positive reinforcement. Positive reinforcement is defined as what managers do after an employee has done something praiseworthy that increases the likelihood they will do it again. Some examples are:
- Praising an employee

- Giving them a bonus or prize
- Thanking an employee
- Recognizing an employee in a meeting

The problem with most managers today is they use negative reinforcement to get employees to do something. This usually takes the form of put-downs, criticism, and sarcasm. I have found that negativity produces negativity. No wonder some businesses have high turnover. Employees hate working there! One researcher found that it takes four positive reinforcements to erase the effect of one negative statement.

Dr. Daniels suggests the following principles about positive reinforcement:

1. What is positive to one employee may not be positive to another.

To help me better understand my employees and what motivates them, I have them fill out a questionnaire at the time of hiring. (See Chapter 3.)

2. The longer we wait to reinforce a behavior the less effect it has. For this reason the manager who works with the employees on a day to day basis is in the best position to influence behavior.

3. One attempt at positive reinforcement with an employee will not make much difference. Positive reinforcement must be constant and consistent.

4. Using the word "but" destroys positive reinforcement. It has been called the sandwich technique - say something good about the employee, then interject the bad with a "but" and then end off with something good. Dr. Daniels says the moment we mix bad with good using "but" we erase positive reinforcement.

I have tried over the past number of years to get out of the "negativity rut". I have found that when I consciously seek to create a positive work environment, the following results occur:
- Employee morale increases
- Employees get along with each other better
- Employees treat my customers better
- Turnover is reduced

Key Points in Chapter Eight

1. The most important factor that builds a positive, motivational atmosphere in a business is how owners and managers treat their employees.

2. Put downs, criticism, and sarcasm do not build employee morale.

3. When we focus on the positive things our employees do, morale increases.

Chapter Nine

Drill Sergeant, Buddy Buddy, Coach?

Much of what we do as managers depends on how we view employee motivation. I define motivation as the physical, mental, and emotional energy an employee brings to the job. Let me illustrate what I mean. I had an employee who was young, good looking and very interested in young women. I could tell when he was motivated and when he was not. For example, when he was helping a middle-aged woman he was unenthused and not too friendly. But when a young college coed was at the counter he was motivated. His physical, mental and emotional energy were focused on one thing - the college coed. That is motivation! Our challenge as employers is to establish an atmosphere in our businesses that encourages our employees to treat all our customers in an exceptional manner.

My experience has taught me this important principle: The way we treat our employees will determine, to a great degree, how they will treat our customers. We can set employee expectations and train them but if we treat them in a negative, rude manner, they will never treat our customers positively.

Yes, perhaps they will be friendly while we are in the store, but when we leave, it is another matter!

Let me here define what to me is real success in managing people: When my employees treat my customers as well when I am not in the store as when I am in the store. The very key is my relationship with my employees.

My relationship with my employees is governed by what I believe about people and how they are motivated. In the previous chapter I discussed the importance of a positive work environment. Some who read this will totally disagree with this. They see employee motivation from an entirely different perspective. There are thousands of business managers in the United States who believe that negative reinforcement is the only type that works.

I am not against reprimanding an employee, but it has been my experience if the atmosphere in our business is usually negative that feeling will carry over to the customer. Negative attitudes usually produce negative employees.

I have found there are three different types of managerial styles. Each style is based on what the manager believes about how people are motivated.

The Drill Sergeant
The Drill Sergeant believes that most people are basically incompetent and that they must constantly be reminded of their responsibilities. This manager manages by intimidation. The dictionary defines intimidation as: to make timid or fearful.

The Drill Sergeant's most effective tool is confrontation. These managers constantly talk down to their employees. They bark orders, threaten employees, and continually look for things employees have done wrong. When the Drill Sergeant walks in, everyone stands at attention. I have asked people in my seminars how many have worked for a boss like this? There are always a number who have. I then ask how this type of boss caused them to feel? Here are some of the responses:

"Like dirt."
"Like I'm worthless."
"Angry."
"Incompetent."
"I want to get back at him."

What the Drill Sergeant is unaware of is how their employees feel about them. The problem is, employees develop no loyalty to this type of manager and they are totally unmotivated do their best at work.

My wife and I live near the ocean and we enjoy walking on the beach. Often, we will stop and look at the sea anemones which are attached to the rocks. They are usually small with wavy tentacles. When you poke sea anemones with your finger or a stick they will immediately close up. They do this to protect themselves from injury. People react the same way when a manager or supervisor pokes them with harshness, negative put-downs or criticism. They close up to protect their self-esteem and to avoid further injury. An employee who has "closed up" is not motivated to do his best. Many, many studies have been done as to how self-esteem affects behavior. They all reveal basically the same thing. When people feel good about themselves they work harder, are happier, and are more motivated. Drill Sergeants should read very carefully Dale Carnegie's book, *How to Win Friends and Influence People.*

The Buddy Buddy

This manager believes that the best way to motivate employees is to be their friend. These managers go out of their way to be nice to their employees. "If people like me, they will work hard for me", they say. While the Drill Sergeant likes confrontation, this is the last thing the Buddy Buddy wants. These managers will avoid confrontation at any cost. Let me illustrate.

Suppose an employee needs to be fired. The Drill Sergeant is up one hour early, the car is running in the driveway, and he speeds all the way to work to fire the employee. But, where is the Buddy Buddy? Still in bed, dreading getting up and dreading the job that needs to be done.

Buddy Buddy managers become such good friends with their employees that there is no real division between their duties. The Buddy Buddy does not want to hurt feelings so employees go undisciplined. This manager will even go so far as to do the job for the employees when it has been left undone.

What is the problem the Buddy Buddy has with employees? You guessed it, employees take advantage of him. It has been amazing to me how fast employees learn how far they can go with their manager. The Buddy Buddy manager does not know how to reprimand or re-direct their employees. They must learn to be tough with their employees in a nice way.

The Coach
Managing people is much like coaching a team. There are the all-stars and the employees that have not yet learned how to play the game. Here are the characteristics of the Coach.

1. The Coach realizes that people are motivated from within and the most a manager can do is establish an atmosphere where employees choose to treat customers well.

2. The Coach believes he/she must earn the respect and loyalty of their employees. The Coach is honest, ethical and realizes that you manage facilities but you lead people. Indeed, leadership is the very key to the Coach's management style. "Do what I say and not what I do," is not in the Coach's vocabulary.

3. The Coach realizes people are different. Some may require a friendlier approach, others may need to be confronted more bluntly and more directly.

4. The Coach seeks to constantly reinforce the good things the employees do. Indeed, this is one of key characteristics of this type of manager.

5. The Coach takes personal responsibility for his/her employees. To accomplish this, the Coach works in the business. The skills discussed in this book are very difficult for an absentee owner to implement. <u>Someone must take</u>

<u>responsibility for what happens in the business and that person must be motivated to care about the business!</u> I have seen some absentee owners accomplish this, but to do it they tied their manager strongly into the business.

It is easy for an owner or manager to get into a negativity rut. Sometimes I have walked into my store and have begun immediately looking for everything my employees have done wrong. When I came to realize the negative effect this had on my employees and then on my customers, I decided to change. To help remind me to be positive, I put a small trash can in the office. On the trash can I put Negative Attitudes. Now, when I go into the store, I throw my negative attitudes into the trash can, and begin looking for the positive things my employees are doing. I sincerely believe that positive treatment of employees leads to positive treatment of customers.

Here is a question that will solidify this idea. I have asked people in my seminars to think of a boss they have had who treated them in such a way that they wanted to do their very best at work. Not one has ever told me that negative remarks and confrontation ever motivated them.
Here are some of the answers:

> "She treated me with respect."
> "He asked for my opinion on things."
> "He allowed for mistakes."
> "She was strict but sensitive to my feelings."
> "He had faith in me. Made me feel like I could do the job."
> "He trained me in the skills I needed to be successful."

Take a moment and answer the same question for yourself. Who has been motivational in your life? What did they do?

Over the years I have seen many managers who have learned how to be a Coach. These managers have acquired certain skills that set them apart from other managers. They have learned the art of creating a positive work environment.

Key Points in Chapter Nine

1. The way we treat our employees will determine, to a great degree, how they treat our customers.

2. Each owner or manager has a style of managing people.

3. The "Drill Sergeant" uses intimidation to influence employees.

4. The "Buddy Buddy" tries to make friends.

5. Neither one of these styles builds a positive work environment.

6. The "Coach" has a sensitivity for people and has learned the skills that create a motivational atmosphere in their business.

Chapter Ten

You Get What You Reward

Consider the following story:

A fisherman was in a boat on a lake fishing. All of a sudden he heard a knock at the side of his boat. He looked and saw a snake with a frog in its mouth. The fisherman immediately felt sorry for the frog, reached down and pulled it out of the snakes mouth. He threw the frog safely over to another part of the lake. He then felt sorry for the snake because he robbed it of its lunch. All he had in his boat was a bottle of whiskey. So, he took the whiskey and gave the snake two shots. The snake swam away and the fisherman went back to fishing. A few minutes later, he heard another knock at the side of his boat. When he looked over he saw the same snake. But this time he had two frogs in its mouth!

What is the message of this story to business owners and managers? You get what you reward!

As discussed previously, experts in the field of behavior motivation say that the most important thing managers can do to motivate employees is create a positive work environment. This idea has powerful implications for how we as small business owners relate with our employees.

I have been making a concentrated effort over the past few years to implement this principle with my employees. For me it has had excellent results. I have lost employees, but the ones I have kept treat our customers well and are more responsible.

Here are examples of specific things you as an owner or manager can do to reinforce the good your employees do. I have divided these ideas into two categories: 1) tangible and 2) intangible rewards.

TANGIBLE REWARDS
1. Money as a reward or incentive.

Money is a powerful incentive for minimum wage employees. It can assist in meeting all four of their needs. Here are some suggestions as to how to use money as a motivator.

a. Raises in pay. A raise in pay means a lot to minimum wage employees. First, it builds their self esteem. It says to them that we feel they are doing a good job and it gives them something to talk about with their friends. Second, it allows them to accomplish some of their immediate goals such as car payments, etc.

There are a couple of ways to make a raise in pay an incentive for our employees.

First, length of time with us. A 10, 15, or 25 cent an hour raise is given at certain time intervals. For example, every three months. When this is communicated to the employee at the time of hiring it can be an incentive to them to stay with us.

Second, for certain accomplishments. A pay raise is given when the employee accomplishes certain tasks that we have established for them. I developed a Customer Service Certified Program for my employees that was based on this idea. (See end of chapter for an example, plus an evaluation for an employee to become Customer Service Certified.)

b. Cash Bonuses. A bonus is a monetary reward for going beyond what is expected or for doing an excellent job at a given task. Here are two examples:

Mystery Shopper Program
If the statement is true, "You get what you reward," then a mystery shopper is one of the best ways to reinforce excellent customer service. Here are some ideas about setting up a mystery shopper program.

- Develop a mystery shopper evaluation. Some areas to consider are:
    Speed of service
    Friendly greeting
    Suggestive selling
    Quality of product
    Grooming of employee
    Sincere thank you

I have the mystery shopper rate the employee on a scale of 1 to 5. You can develop this form yourself using the above areas. See example at the end of this chapter.

- Inform all employees about the Mystery Shopper program. Let them see the form the mystery shopper will use to evaluate them.
- Establish a bonus for employees who score a pre-determined number of points on the evaluation.
- Talk with friends and customers and ask them to be a mystery shopper. Clearly explain to them the evaluation form and what they are to look for. They are to get a receipt for their transaction and when they return it with the evaluation, they are refunded the price of the transaction.
- Display very good evaluations in the employee area of the business. Poor evaluations are not displayed but the employee is shown the evaluation and talked with.

Customer feedback

Another way to offer bonuses is through customer feedback. I do not use the standard card that some fast food restaurants have sitting on their tables. The reason being that the only people who take time to fill it out are Ms. Smiley, Mr. Grumpy, and the friends of the employee. What I prefer to do is to have a customer response week. I do this two or three times a year. Here is how it works:

- For one week our employees hand a customer response card to each customer. They say the following: " We appreciate your business and want to know how we are doing. Please take 30 seconds to fill this out and drop it in the box as you leave. Next week we will have a drawing from those who have responded and the winner will receive _____."

- The response card looks like this:

We value your opinion
Please rate us Poor (P), Average (A), Superior (S)

Friendliness of Employees	P A S
Speed of Service	P A S
Quality of Product	P A S
Cleanliness of Store	P A S
Price of Product	P A S

Should we receive 90 percent superior responses, every employee receives a cash bonus.

2. Plaque, Certificate, Note

The Boy and Girl Scout programs are based on badges and most young people will do anything for a badge.

Anytime we can recognize one of our employees it reinforces their self-esteem. Here are some ideas for rewards:

The Golden Ear Award - for employees who listen well to customers.

The Silver Tongue Award - for employees who are friendly with customers.

The ABCD Award - for behavior Above, Beyond, the Call of Duty.

The Team Builder Award - for an employee who is supportive of other team or crew members.

Another way to recognize an employee is to put a note in their pay check envelope. The note could be a recognition of something specific the employee did. For example:

- Putting the customer first
- Taking the initiative
- Making the workplace fun
- Being responsible

Awards could be given out at a team or crew meeting. Here are some suggestions for conducting a team meeting

Team or Crew Meetings

One of the best ways to build a positive team feeling is to hold periodic team meetings. Here are some suggestions:

1. Hold the meeting away from the place of work. Our team meetings are held at a nearby restaurant. I provide breakfast for my employees and the owner of the restaurant gives me 20% off the bill.
2. The meeting should be upbeat and fun. This is not the time to come down on employees.
3. The meeting should last no longer than forty-five minutes to an hour.
4. Plan ahead for the team meeting. Here is a typical agenda for one of our team meetings:
    A. Meet at 8:00 AM
    B. Order breakfast
    C. Training on some aspect of the business
       - 10 minutes

D. Review of upcoming promotions
E. Operations items
F. Employee suggestions

Possibly one of the most important items of the meeting is employee suggestions. I simply ask our employees, "What suggestions do you have to make our business better?" I listen and take notes and comment as needed.

3. Prizes/Contests
Sometimes a reward can be in the form of a prize. Young people respond well to this type of positive reinforcement. Let's look at two ways to do this.

Individual Rewards
Individual rewards can be given for many different things that employees do. Sometimes a reward may be given to motivate an employee to do something that is a part of their job description such as, being on time to work, consistently wearing the proper uniform, or performing a task that the employee has had a problem with.

Rewards may also be given when an employee goes beyond what is expected. For example:
- Selling so many or so much of a given product
- Getting a job done in a certain amount of time

When I was a teenager my Dad began manufacturing and selling "Chicken Legs." Chicken legs were made by putting a special ground meat rolled in corn flakes on a stick in the shape of a chicken leg. My job was to put the ground meat on the stick. Dad paid me by the hour and he would motivate me by offering a bonus if I could do so many in an hour. I remember well how it became a real challenge for me to beat my previous record. Competing against myself, along with the bonus, were enough to motivate me to perform to the best of my ability.

The very key to individual rewards is knowing what it is that motivates each of your employees. Some like competition. Therefore, a contest such as who can sell the most of a given product, is fun. Others do not like competition. One manager I know capitalized on this idea to motivate one of his supervisors to go beyond his normal performance. He told the supervisor that if he could accomplish a job in a certain amount of time, he would give him two tickets to the next pro-football game. The supervisor was into sports and accomplished the job in nearly half the time it would normally take him. The manager learned two things: first, positive reinforcement works, and second, the supervisor could perform much better than expected. What did the supervisor learn? He could do much more than he thought he could. Now, the manager gives that supervisor an incentive every few months and the supervisor looks forward to the challenge.

Here are some examples of different types of prizes:
- Ticket to movies, concerts or sporting events
- Trinkets - coffee mug, Mickey Mouse watch
- Gift certificate
- Baseball cap with logo, sweatshirt, tee-shirt
- Compact Disc

Team Awards

Reward team members for reaching a specified sales volume. Hand out customer satisfaction cards for one week. If the average response is good to excellent then the team members get a reward. A certain percentages can be rewarded. For example in the food business if food costs are kept at a certain percentage for a month the team is rewarded.

Here are two guidelines:
>Only reward employees for things within their control. If they have no control over the outcome there is no motivation.
>
>A contest can lose its punch if it is conducted over a long period of time. One month is usually long enough!

INTANGIBLE REWARDS
1. Praise them! Praise them! Praise them!

I have found that praising an employee for doing things right is one of the most important things I can do. Instead of trying to catch them doing things wrong, I make an effort to catch them doing things right. What a difference this makes! For example, when I see an employee handle an upset customer in a professional manner, I compliment that employee.

"Kathy, you did a great job dealing with that upset customer. Keep up the good work!"

I have made a list of the right things I want my employees doing. When I am in the store I look for these things, so that I can reinforce that positive behavior. Here are some of the examples from my list:

>Positive things to look for
>- Being well groomed and dressed properly

- Greeting customers in a friendly manner
- Being friendly and talking with customers
- Thanking customers
- Dealing well with a customer's problem
- Doing tasks without being asked
- Opening or closing the store properly
- Always having a positive attitude while at work

I have also learned some principles relative to praising employees.

    a. It must be sincere. You must sincerely believe that praising the employee is important, otherwise it will come off as insincere.

    b. It must be merited. You must make sure the employee actually did something for which to be praised.

    c. It should be as specific as possible. Note the difference in the following:

        Manager A - "I like the way you treat our customers."

        Manager B - "I like the way you always smile and greet our customers in such a friendly manner.

The more specific your praise, the clearer it is to the employee what you want them to continue doing.

    d. Praise the employee as soon as possible. The longer you wait to praise after the employee has done something right, the less effect it will have.

    e. Remember, praise in public, reprimand in private.

    f. Praise can also be communicated in written form. A note in the pay check envelope might read, "Thanks for covering Jim's shift last week. Keep up the great work!".

g. Call the parent of the employee and let him/her know the great job their son/daughter is doing.

2. Ask for Their Opinion

Employees feel more positive about their job and their boss when they are asked to give their opinion on a matter. Every so often I will ask an employee "What could we do better in our store?". Another way is to present them with a problem and ask for their opinion. For example, "Our night crew is just not keeping the store clean. What do you think could be done to change that?".

I have also used an employee feedback form. This is used once every three to four months. Employees are asked to fill it out anonymously. See example at the end of this chapter.

3. Employee Evaluation

One of the most positive ways to reinforce good behavior and to change negative behavior is through an employee evaluation. I evaluate our employees once every quarter. The evaluation usually takes 10-15 minutes. Here is how I do it:

a. Develop an employee evaluation form that addresses the particular points of the business. I focus especially on customer service. See example at the end of this chapter.

b. Set a time for the evaluation that is convenient for the employee.

c. Give the evaluation to the employee before the meeting and ask them to rate themself.

d. At the appointed time I sit down with the employee and review their evaluation and make my own observations. At the end, employees set a goal for themselves for the next 3 months.

4. Use of Positive Reminders

I try to do little things that remind my employees of the importance of our customers. Here are some ideas:

    a. Hang motivational signs in the employee area of the store. Some of my favorites are:

        " You never get a second chance to make a good first impression."

        "The customer may not always be right, but they are the customer."

        "Keep smiling! It communicates we care."

    b. Stamp pay envelopes every pay period with the following: "Our customers made this check possible."

    c. Have a bulletin board to post signs and written messages:

        "Happy birthday Jill", "Great close Craig"

5. Allow Employees to Make Decisions

Oftentimes as a boss or manager we make all the decisions. Employees who have a degree of flexibility in making decisions feel better about their job. Let them know specifically what they can and cannot do. For example, if a customer is upset, what is the employee allowed to do? Giving them the right to make decisions is very motivating.

6. Allow Employees to Make Mistakes

I have to constantly remind myself that most of my employees are young and do not have the experience I have. When we continually come down on our employees, not allowing for mistakes, we condition them to fail.

When I was in high school I played on our football team. We had a punter who had a problem kicking the ball off the side of his foot. As he would enter the game to punt the ball, our coach would invariably say, "Don't kick the ball off the side of your foot!" What image did our punter have in his mind as he kicked the ball? Wouldn't it have been better for our coach to have given him positive reinforcement? "Kick the ball high and straight. I know you can do it!" Do you see the difference?

7. Admit Your Own Mistakes

When we as owners and managers admit our mistakes, we create an open atmosphere where our employees are more willing to communicate and accept responsibility for their own mistakes. If we consistently blame others and shift responsibility, so will our employees.

Giving employees tangible and intangible rewards creates a positive work environment. Granted, there are some people who are self-motivated and perhaps do not need as much attention. But the majority of our employees will need our concern and our encouragement.

Here is the lesson I have learned managing people:

"Take care of your employees and they will take care of your business."

Customer Service Certified

Name _____ Hire Date _____

Starting Wage _____

Step 1 - Two Week Orientation
To be completed within two weeks of hire
1. Understanding of Expectations studied and signed   _____
2. Team Rules and Disciplinary Policy Studied/Signed   _____
3. Secret Shopper form studied   _____
4. Employee training videos watched and
   workbook completed   _____
5. Customer Service Quick Start Cards Memorized   _____
   Completion Date _____   Wage Increase _____

Step 2 - Read 4 chapters in *How to Win Friends and Influence People*
To be completed within three weeks of hire
   Completion Date _____   Wage Increase _____

Step 3 - Customer Service Certified
To be completed within one month of hire. Evaluation completed by owner/manager.   _____
   Completion Date _____   Wage Increase _____

Employee Evaluation for Becoming "Customer Service Certified"

Employee _____ Date _____

Evaluator's Name _____

Instructions:
In each category circle the number for the statement that best describes the behavior or attitude of the employee. Please make a rating for each item.

The total possible points an employee can receive from this evaluation is 36. To become Customer Service Certified an employee must achieve 30 or more points.

1. Attitude toward customers: _____
    1. Inconsiderate/Indifferent
    2. Polite but reserved
    3. Warm, friendly, outgoing

2. Friendly greeting of customers: _____
    1. Rarely looks up when customers enter
    2. Occasionally
    3. Always welcomes customers

3. Talks with customers: _____
    1. Rarely
    2. Occasionally
    3. Always

Employee Evaluation for Becoming "Customer Service Certified" (Cont.)

4. Says "Thank You" and smiles: _____

    1. Rarely
    2. Occasionally
    3. Always

5. Quality of product: _____
    1. Poor
    2. Average
    3. Above average

6. Suggestive selling: _____

    1. Rarely
    2. Occasionally
    3. Always

7. Commitment to job: _____
    1. Shows a lack of real commitment
    2. Does an average job but lacks commitment to superior performance
    3. Dedicated commitment to work and does a thorough job

8. Doing more than minimum for customers: _____
    1. Not helpful: tends to be rude and impatient
    2. Friendly but needs to develop "put customers first" attitude
    3. Consistently gives more than the minimum to customers

9. Accuracy of performance: _____
    1. Very careless and sloppy performance

Employee Evaluation for Becoming "Customer Service Certified" (Cont.)

     2.   Tends to be inaccurate and occasionally makes mistakes
     3.   Careful and consistently accurate

10. Handles customer complaints well: _____
     1.   Rarely
     2.   Occasionally
     3.   Always

11. Answers telephone courteously: _____
     1.   Rarely
     2.   Occasionally
     3.   Always

12. Speed of service: _____
     1.   Slow
     2.   Fairly fast
     3.   Very fast

TOTAL POINTS _____

Should an employee receive less than 30 points the employee can be reevaluated in 2 weeks. Set specific goals for improvement during that two-week period.

Employee Evaluation

Performance Period
First 30 days from _____ to _____   Employee _____
After 90 days from _____ to _____   Job title _____
After 6 months from _____ to _____   Today's date _____

A. CUSTOMER SERVICE
Attitude toward customers _____
Comments:
1. Indifferent _____
2. Polite but reserved _____
3. Warm, friendly _____

Initial contact with customers
1. Rarely smiles _____
2. Occasionally smiles _____
3. Always smiles _____

Use of customer name
1. Doesn't use names _____
2. Tries sometimes _____
3. Always tries _____

Thanks customer
1. Rarely _____
2. Sometimes _____
3. Always _____

Quality of product served
1. Seldom ensures quality _____
2. Usually ensures quality _____
3. Always serves quality product

Employee Evaluation (cont.)

Overall communication with customer

1. Negative _____
2. Fair _____
3. Positive _____

B. ATTITUDE TOWARD JOB
Reliability toward job

1. Rarely follows through _____
2. Tries _____
3. Always follows through _____

Punctuality

1. Frequently late _____
2. Usually on time _____
3. Always _____

Initiative

1. Does less than asked _____
2. Does only what is asked _____
3. Does more than asked _____

Personal appearance, grooming

1. Seldom neat and tidy _____
2. Usually neat and tidy _____
3. Always _____

Employee Evaluation (cont.)

C. TEAMWORK/STORE ATMOSPHERE
Attitude toward co-workers

1. Poor _____
2. Good _____
3. Excellent _____

Overall efforts to help co-workers

1. Poor - usually has to be asked _____
2. Good _____
3. Excellent _____

Attitude toward management

1. Resentful/indifferent _____
2. Helpful _____
3. Motivated _____

Sensitive to store cleanliness

1. Seldom take initiative _____
2. Usually _____
3. Always takes initiative _____

Follows instructions

1. Doesn't follow _____
2. Usually follows _____
3. Always follows _____

Employee Evaluation (cont.)

D. HANDLING CUSTOMER COMPLAINTS
Ability to deal with customer complaints
1. Gets defensive
2. Not sure how to handle _____
3. Effective at dealing with _____

Shows empathy to customer
1. Rarely _____
2. Does not know how _____
3. Knows how to listen _____

Takes responsibility
1. Blames others _____
2. Turns customer over
   to someone else _____
3. Handles the complaint _____

E. SALESMANSHIP
Uses techniques for upselling
1. Rarely _____
2. Sometimes _____
3. Always _____

Uses techniques for suggestive selling
1. Rarely _____
2. Sometimes _____
3. Always _____

Employee Evaluation (cont.)

GOAL FOR EMPLOYEE IMPROVEMENT

_____
_____
_____
_____
_____
_____
_____
_____

Example of a Mystery Shopper Form

Store Address _____ Time of Visit _____
Employee Name _____ # of Customers in Store _____
# of Employees in store _____
# of Customers Ahead of you in line _____

Quality of Product
5 = Excellent   4 = Very Good   3 = Good   2 = Needs Improvement   1 = Poor

1.	The bread looked fresh and golden brown 1	2	3	4	5
2.	The sandwich was made exactly as you ordered 1	2	3	4	5
	List any differences _____				
3.	The vegetables looked fresh 1	2	3	4	5
4.	The sandwich tasted 1	2	3	4	5

Total Points _____

Comments
_____
_____
_____
_____

Customer Service

1.	You were greeted promptly with a smile	1	2	3	4	5
2.	The employees were well groomed and in full uniform	1	2	3	4	5
3.	Employee washed hands and wore gloves	1	------------------------			5
4.	Employee was friendly	1	2	3	4	5
5.	Employee suggested other products	1	2	3	4	5
6.	Employee said "Thank you" and made you feel he/she cared about your business	1	2	3	4	5
7.	Speed of service	1	2	3	4	5
8.	Store was clean - tables, floors	1	2	3	4	5

Total Points _____

Example of a Mystery Shopper Form (cont.)

Comments

_____
_____
_____
_____
_____

OVERALL

Your overall experience at our business was   1   2   3   4   5

                                                                                   Total

Points _____

Comments

_____
_____
_____
_____

                         Total All 3 Categories _____

Total Possible Points = 65
     60-65 Excellent
     55-60 Good

Employee Feedback - Tell Us What You Think

Please answer the following questions by circling either "Strongly Agree" (SA), "Agree" (A), "Uncertain" (U), "Disagree" (D), or "Strongly Disagree" (SD).

1. SA A U D SD — My manager handles every day stress well.
2. SA A U D SD — My manager sets an example of excellence in the store.
3. SA A U D SD — Reprimands are not given when they should be.
4. SA A U D SD — I like the management.
5. SA A U D SD — Management communicates well with employees.
6. SA A U D SD — The manager of this store works hard and does his/her fair share.
7. SA A U D SD — I was not trained adequately to perform my duties.
8. SA A U D SD — Our manager treats everyone like equals.
9. SA A U D SD — It is easy for employees to take care of customer complaints.
10. SA A U D SD — Customer service is a high priority and is emphasized in this store on a regular basis.
11. SA A U D SD — I enjoy talking with customers.
12. SA A U D SD — This store delivers excellent customer service on a regular basis.
13. SA A U D SD — Employees never talk about personal issues while on the front line.
14. SA A U D SD — I have positive feelings about this company.
15. SA A U D SD — This company offers opportunities to those employees who want to advance.
16. SA A U D SD — The expectations this company places on each employee are reasonable.
17. SA A U D SD — I am able to express my views for improving operations in the store.
18. SA A U D SD — This company's policies and procedures are fair.
19. SA A U D SD — I am motivated to do a great job for my store.
20. SA A U D SD — Most employees have a strong sense of loyalty to this store.

21.	SA	A	U	D	SD	We are recognized for extra effort and dedication.
22.	SA	A	U	D	SD	I enjoy my job.
23.	SA	A	U	D	SD	Cleanliness at this store is important to me.
24.	SA	A	U	D	SD	The employees at this store are honest and never steal or give things away to friends.
25.	SA	A	U	D	SD	Most employees waste a lot of time.
26.	SA	A	U	D	SD	Employees always pay for merchandise.
27.	SA	A	U	D	SD	A quality product is very important here.
28.	SA	A	U	D	SD	I am expected to do too much during my shift.
29.	SA	A	U	D	SD	If I could find another job at the same pay, I would leave my job.

Short Answer

One thing I would like to get off my mind is . . .

_____
_____
_____
_____
_____

If I were the manager I would change . . .

_____
_____
_____
_____

Key Points in Chapter Ten

1. Rewarding employees for the positive things they do is a powerful way to influence their behavior.

2. There are two types of rewards: tangible, like money and prizes, or intangible, like praise and recognition.

3. When we take care of our employees, they take care of our business.

Chapter Eleven

Turning Problem Employees Around

One day, while sitting in my office, one of our best employees came to me and said, "Could I talk with you a minute?"

I said, "Sure, what can I do for you?"

The employee said, "I think I'm going to look for another job."

"What's the problem?"

"I'm not enjoying my job. It used to be fun working here, but not anymore."

There, staring me in the face, was the number one concern of every business owner I have known, TURNOVER! Some industries estimate that each time an employee quits or is fired it costs the owner of the business over $1000.00.

I have to admit that I have lost some employees because of my neglect in hiring and training properly. Others, because I did not invest the time to create a positive environment in my business. Other employees have their own problems that have nothing to do with me. My challenge then is to try and turn these employees around. Herein lies one of the greatest challenges we face managing people, assisting them in changing their negative behavior.

Often managers look upon correction of an employee's poor performance as one of the nastiest aspects of their job. Particularly is this true for the Buddy Buddy manager. He/she wants to avoid confrontation at all costs!

However, correcting an employee can be viewed as one of the most important aspects of a manager's job. Here is why. The word "discipline" refers to those positive habits that people acquire which make life more enjoyable. Most would agree that when an employee has the discipline to be to work on time their job will be more enjoyable. An employee who disciplines himself to keep his cool with an upset customer will have greater control over the situation. A manager's major responsibility is to assist his/her employees in developing discipline so that they enjoy their job more. As I said earlier, we are in the business of developing people!

A second reason managers do not like correcting employees is that it is not easy and often turns out disastrous. It requires skill to assist an employee in changing their behavior. Here are some of the most common areas where employees need help in learning discipline.
- Treating customers properly
- Arriving to work on time
- Wearing proper work uniform
- Personal hygiene
- Getting along with other employees

Dealing with these and a host of other employee problems is challenging. But a manager must deal with them or risk losing customers, lowering employee morale, and losing respect.

There is one point every manager needs to understand up front. We simply cannot turn around every problem employee we hire! In spite of all of our efforts to hire and train properly, to reinforce in a positive manner the good they do, and to discipline in a proper manner, some employees will simply not respond. It reminds me of the story of the frog and the scorpion.

A frog was sitting at the edge of the river when a scorpion came up to him and said, "I need to get to the other side of the river. Could you carry me across?"

The frog replied, "No way! You'll probably sting me if I carry you across!"

The scorpion said, "Why would I do that? We then would both drown."

The frog decided to assist the scorpion but half way across the river the scorpion stung the frog. As they both were going under for the last time, the frog said, "Why did you do that? Now we both will die!"

The scorpion replied, "I guess it's just in my nature!"

Out of the many employees I have hired, about 25% have just not had it in their nature to do the job I expected. Because of their immaturity they had not yet chosen to be responsible and to change what they needed to change. However, learning to properly discipline can help turn around problem employees and reduce turnover. So, let's look at how to do it!

One author has suggested that managers need to avoid "seven deadly sins" when disciplining employees. I agree with each of these "sins".

1. Failing to obtain all the relevant facts and disciplining based on only hearsay evidence.

2. Disciplining the employee when one is emotionally out of control. This entails losing one's temper and "flying off the handle".

3. Failing to let the employee know the precise reason he or she is being disciplined.

4. Failing to get the employee's side of the story and not letting him or her talk.

5. Letting the employee talk you out of the punishment that should rightly be invoked.

6. Failing to document what transpires during the disciplinary interview.

7. Holding a grudge against the employee after the disciplinary interview and reminding him or her either verbally or nonverbally about it.

[L.L. Steinmetz, *Managing the Marginal and Unsatisfactory Performer*, 2nd ed. (Reading, MA: Addison - Wesley Publishing, 1985)]

I would add an eighth sin to this list:
8. Disciplining an employee in front of customers or other employees.

Here are my five steps to turning problem employees around. My ultimate goal is to help the employee change so that I don't lose him or her. Turnover is costly. I try and do all I can to turn the employee around before taking serious action. Again, I have set up the following progressive steps in disciplining employees. The steps go along with the Team Rules and Discipline form in Chapter 6. Each of these steps is to correct a serious or less serious violation.

Step 1 - A verbal reminder
Step 2 - A sit-down face-to-face talk with the employee. If I feel the employee is not adequate for the job I may skip this step and go right to steps 3 or 4. I have, however, turned many employees around with this face-to-face talk.
Step 3 - Written warning
Step 4 - Reduction of hours or some form of negative result
Step 5 - Termination

I have found that most of my employees who were willing to change did so at Step 2, the sit-down face-to-face talk. However, a few employees did not change until I gave them a written warning.

By the time I get to Step 4, reduction of work hours, the employee quits, relieving me of the responsibility of firing them.

I have had managers ask me, "What do we do if an employee is good in most areas but just won't change in one ?"

My response has been that they need to carefully weigh how valuable the employee is. If you can live with the problem area then continue to encourage them to change but keep them.

Now, let's look at each of these steps.
Step 1 - Verbal Reminder

A verbal Reminder may do one of two things:
1. Redirect an employee who has not yet learned to do what you want. This is used particularly with new employees. Here is what you can say:

> "Maybe I wasn't clear when I hired you."
> "Perhaps I failed to mention..."
> "Let's review what I expect."
> "Let's review how to..."

2. Reprimand an employee who knows what to do but has failed to do it. Try to relate the employee's behavior to the effect it has on customers. Here are some examples:

"You forgot to thank the customer. Thanking the customer lets them know we appreciate their business."

"Remember to look at our customers when you greet them.

It says we care."

After a verbal reprimand make sure the employee knows you still value him/her.
> "I know you'll do better."
> "I have confidence in you."
> "You're better than this."

Step 2 - Face-to-face sit down talk - Manager/Supervisor makes a record of the discussion

   A. Describe specifically what the employee did and what problems his/her behavior created.

   B. Invite the employee to give an explanation for his/her behavior.

   C. Invite the employee to offer a specific solution for his/her behavior problem.

   C. Describe clearly the consequences for the employee:
      a. Following through
      b. Not following through

   E. Fill out and sign the Verbal Counseling Form. These forms are found at the back of this chapter

An Example Of A Face-to-Face Sit-Down Talk
The following experience actually happened. By using the steps discussed in this chapter the employee became very good at customer service and stayed with us for over a year.

The problem: John had been with us for about two weeks when it became evident that he was inconsistent when it came to customer service. Some days he was friendly and others he was cold and distant. We set up a time to talk and I went through the five steps.

A. - Describe specifically what the employee did and what problems his/her behavior created.

Bob: "You know how important customer service is to our business. I have encouraged you to be friendly with our customers. However, some days you are friendly and others you are cold to our customers. You don't smile or act at all friendly. Your behavior creates a problem for my business. Customers do not feel you care."

B. - Invite an explanation.

Bob: "Do you have anything to say about this?"

John: "I wasn't aware I was unfriendly."

Bob: "Well, some days you just seem to be cold."

John: "I have to admit that with school and everything, sometimes I just don't feel like being friendly."

Bob: "I'm paying you to be friendly."

C. - Seek a specific solution

Bob: "What could you do to be friendly when you don't feel like it?"

John: "Are you suggesting that I put on an act?"

Bob: "That's a great idea, John. When you don't feel friendly you will act like you are friendly. Most of the work done in this country is done by people who don't feel good! This will be a great lesson for you. Can you do it?"

John: "I'll try."

D. - Describe the consequences.
Bob: "Well, if you can treat our customers in a friendly manner especially when you don't feel like it, you'll have a job here. If I see the behavior doesn't change I'll give you a written warning and reduce your hours. Are these consequences clear?"

John: "Yes."

Bob: "Do you have any questions?"

John: "No, I'll try to be more friendly."

E. – After this meeting, fill out the Verbal Counseling Form.

Step 3 – Written Warning
    1. Begin the meeting by telling the employee that he/she is being given a Written Warning.
    2. Show the employee the Written Warning form and allow him/her to read it.
    3. Refer to the verbal counseling form and review it with the employee especially noting point C which refers to what the employee had agreed to do.
    4. Listen to the employee's response.
    5. Tell the employee the specific behavior you expect.
    6. Develop a plan to correct the employee's behavior

clearly explaining that failure to follow through this time will result in a reduction of hours or termination.

7. Sign the warning form and ask the employee to also sign it.

8. Indicate your confidence that the employee's behavior will change.

Learning to turn problem employees around is a skill we learn. We are certainly not born with it! Over the years I have used the above tools to help me keep those employees who were willing to change. Perhaps one of the most gratifying experiences I have had is to see the growth that occurs as my employees become the type of people that will help them become successful in life.

The efforts we make to turn a problem employee around can be very rewarding. First, turnover, which is very costly, will be reduced. Second, we will assist the people we hire in becoming more responsible.

Verbal Counseling Form

Employee (print)_____ **Store** _____

Manager _____ **Date**_____

A. Describe the employee's unsatisfactory performance.

B. What explanation did the employee give for his/her performance?

C. What solution to the problem did the employee give?

D. What consequences were explained to the employee?

   Manager's signature _____

Written Warning Form

Employee (print) _____ **Date** _____

Violation
- ❏ Late for work
- ❏ Absenteeism
- ❏ Dress Code
- ❏ Not Following Policy
- ❏ Poor Customer Service
- ❏ Rude Behavior
- ❏ Telephone Calls
- ❏ Other

Date of violation _____

1. What occurred - where, when, how:

2. Employee comments:

3. Action to be taken if violation occurs again:

   Manager's signature _____

   Employee's signature _____

Key Points in Chapter Eleven

1. One of the most important aspects of managing a business is turning problem employees around because turn over is costly.

2. This is not always easy as some employees are just not willing to change.

3. Establishing team rules and a discipline policy at the time of hiring, can help in the process of turning problem employees around.

4. Managers must realize that they will need to constantly work with the behavior of their employees.

5. One of the most effective ways to turn a problem employee around is a sit down, face to face talk.

Chapter Twelve

Safety and Security

A book on managing employees would not be complete without some discussion about safety and security. The safety of not only our customers, but our employees, and security as it relates to one of the greatest problems in American business today - employee theft.

First, customer and employee safety. Two stories will illustrate the importance of a manager's concern for this area.

In one of our stores, we had an outside eating area. We placed umbrellas in the tables to protect customers from the sun. The umbrellas were brought into the store at night to avoid theft. In the morning, our opening employee was to put the umbrellas out in the tables. One morning the employee neglected to do so and a customer came into the store to order a sandwich. The umbrellas were still up against the side of the counter. You guessed it! One of the umbrellas fell, striking the customer on the side of the head. After months of doctor and hospital visits, you can imagine the cost of that employee mistake! Fortunately, I had liability insurance, but I still had to pay the deductible.

A second story happened to a business associate of mine. He had scheduled a young woman employee to close the store. At eleven at night, a man came into the store, grabbed the young woman and took her to the back of the store. He raped her and stole what money he could get. The employee not only sued the owner of the store but the owner of the franchise for neglect in the area of employee safety. Her lawsuit was one of the largest ever awarded in that state.

The point of these two stories is evident. As business owners and managers we must be committed to safety. Here are some suggestions:

1. Customer safety.

The first suggestion is to make sure you have adequate liability insurance. Without this, I would never open my doors for business!

Next, look for places or areas in your business where potential problems are just waiting to happen. It may be slippery floors, objects such as plants that are hanging from the ceiling, or places in the parking lot where customers may trip or fall.

Develop a checklist for employees as to what they should do if a customer has a problem. The key question to ask is, "What could possibly happen to my customers?" Then, make the necessary corrections to see that those things do not happen.

2. Employee safety.

Every industry has common employee safety problems. A safety problem is anything that affects the personal well-being of our employees. For example, in the fast food industry the following are common: Skin cuts from knives, meat and vegetable slicers; burns from grills and deep-fat fryers; back problems from lifting inventory; and leg problems from long hours of standing.

Another safety problem that seems to be increasing is criminal acts. Robbery is one of the most common safety issues in large cities. Another area is that of disaster preparedness. What do employees do in case of a fire, electrical shut down, or other unforeseen acts of nature? Sexual harassment is also an area that we need to be concerned about. What can we do to ensure the safety of our employees and to avoid liability as owners and managers? While I am not a legal expert in this area, I do recommend the following:

First, make sure that the proper health and safety signs are posted in the employee work or break area. Many of these notices are mandated by the government. If you are not sure which signs should be displayed, contact your local labor board and OSHA.

Second, make a list of potential employee safety problems for your particular business. This list will vary according to the business you are in. It might include some of those I have suggested above.

Third, develop a checklist that clearly outlines to the employees what they should and should not do. For example, what should an employee do and not do if an individual is trying to rob the store? What should employees do if they feel that they are being sexually harassed? What should employees do to avoid back injury? Etc.

Fourth, make sure that employees read the health and safety guidelines and have them sign and date a form that signifies they have read the material. These signed papers then go into the employee's individual file.

Fifth, include in your new employee training a section on health and safety issues. The business environment we are now living in makes this absolutely essential. I have another business associate who owns a number of fast food restaurants. One of his employees sued him because she said she was sexually harassed by one of his managers. He won the lawsuit. Or did he? It cost him $15,000 to win the lawsuit!

Employee Theft

Employee theft costs business owners billions of dollars each year. That's right! I said billions, not millions. It was estimated that in 1995, 40% of all business failures in the United States were because of employee theft. How do we as business owners and managers allow this to happen? For myself, I have always believed that the people I hired were honest. I changed my thinking after one of my managers stole over $2000 from me. How did she do it? She sold product and pocketed the money.

I should have been a smarter business owner. Particularly because of a lesson I should have learned from my Dad when I was about fifteen. My Dad now owned a very successful meat processing plant and he serviced local restaurants with meat products, etc. One evening at about nine o'clock, we went to the plant, entered the back door, and, with the aid of a flashlight, went to the large freezer that held all of the frozen products. My Dad counted all of the boxes and then did a very strange thing. He took a piece of thread out of his pocket, attached it to one side of the door jam and then to the other. We then left the freezer making sure we stepped over the thread. I had some idea that he was concerned someone was stealing from him. The next morning we went to the plant very early. Dad opened the freezer door and found the thread was broken. He then counted the inventory and found some missing. He called around and found that his driver was selling product on the side and pocketing the money. The driver was my Dad's very best friend! He had known him for years and had hired him thinking that friends don't steal from friends. Here is the lesson I should have learned: Always assume that employees are stealing, never assume they are not!

One study of employee theft indicated the following:
- 20 percent of all employees are likely to steal
- 20 percent won't steal no matter what the opportunity
- 60 percent will steal if they find the risk to be minimal

What do employers do to make it easy for employees to steal?
1. They have ineffective security systems.
2. They have poor controls for handling money and for accounting for inventory.

3. They have no system for checking on employees.

What can we do to minimize employee theft?

First, use a pre-employment honesty test. As indicated before, this test will tell you how likely it is that an employee, if given the opportunity, will steal from you.

Second, explain to each employee at the time of hiring what your expectations are relative to honesty. This might include specific directions as to food they can eat without charge or discounts they receive as an employee. Also explain to them the consequences should they be dishonest.

Third, develop systems to check daily inventory that comes in and products that are sold. Most businesses have certain key items that can be checked to determine if what was sold equals the money that was taken in. Modern cash registers and computers now track such things and are well worth the expense.

Fourth, work in the business to insure what is happening. Often it is the absentee owner or the multi-unit owner who are not aware of what is going on in their businesses. Daily spot checks by an owner are essential to discourage theft.

Fifth, should your business be conducive to employee theft, install a video monitoring system. These are available in most areas for a relatively nominal fee. This system is a great deterrent to employee theft and to robbery.

Perhaps, one final word should be said. Not only do we need to worry about employees ripping us off, we need to be concerned about our customers ripping us off. Our son-in-law purchased a franchised printing shop. A customer came in and ordered a $3,000 project that required my son-in-law to contract out part of the work. He had to pay $1700 up front for the work he contracted out. You probably know where this story is going. The customer's $500 deposit check bounced and my son-in-law to this day has never been able to find him. What is the moral of this story? Never, never do anything for a customer that requires an outlay of cash on your part, without receiving the cash up front from the customer.

There is one motto that every business owner and manager should live by: "If it can happen, it will." The problems occur when we assume it will never happen to us. A little planning and prevention up front is worth, as someone said, "a pound of cure later on."

Key points in Chapter Twelve

1. A high priority of owners and managers should be the safety of customers and employees.

2. A good liability policy is essential.

3. Employees need to be trained in safety procedures and they need to sign a form indicating they have received the training.

4. Required signs need to be posted where employees can see them.

5. We must assume that employees will try and steal from us.

6. Controls need to be established to deter employee theft.

Conclusion

Perhaps as you have read this book you have felt overwhelmed. Maybe you are not sure where to start. Maybe you wonder how you can apply what I have written.

Someone once asked, "How do you eat an elephant?" The answer, "one bite at a time." So it is with learning how to manage minimum wage employees. Begin with the idea that you feel is most needed right now in your business.

Below is a summary of each of the major ideas in this book. At the left is a box. Place in the box a 1 2, 3, etc. according to which idea you will apply first, second and so on.

☐ Step 1 — Determine what you expect of your employees. What type of behavior do you want them to demonstrate?

☐ Step 2 – Learn to effectively interview potential employees. Develop a list of open-ended questions. Listen with your eyes as well as your ears.

☐ Step 3 – Set employee expectations at the very beginning. Be as specific as possible. Put your expectations in writing.

☐ Step 4 - Develop a team rules and discipline form.

☐ Step 5 – Determine what skills your employees need and develop specific checklists to train them in the areas you want them to be proficient in.

☐ Step 6 – Develop a positive work environment by using tangible and intangible rewards. Select one idea to reinforce the good your employees do.

☐ Step 7 – Coach your crew members on a daily basis focusing on employees who are not measuring up. Sit down in a face-to-face talk with problem employees.

☐ Step 8 – Develop safety and security procedures and train all employees to follow them.

These eight steps will not by any means solve every problem you might encounter with minimum wage employees. But as you put them into practice I can assure you the following results:
- You will enjoy your job more.
- Employees will have greater respect for you.
- Customer service will increase.
- A more positive -- and profitable -- atmosphere will be created in your business.

The story is told of a town many years ago that had an old, wise man who could answer any question that anybody in the town had. Two teenagers, wanting to prove that the sage was not as wise as everyone thought, devised a plan. They would find a small bird, one of the teenagers would put it in his hand, and walk up to the old, wise man. He would then say, "We've come here to find out how wise you are. I have a bird in my hand. Is it alive or is it dead?" If the old, wise man said it was dead, the teenager would open his hands and let it fly away. If the wise man said it was alive, the teenager would crush it and say, "No, you're not as wise as everyone thinks!"

So, the teenagers found a small bird and went in search of the old, wise man. They found him in the town square, sitting on a bench meditating. One of the teenagers walked up to the old man and extending his hand, said, "We have come here to find out how wise you are. I have a bird in my hand. Is it alive or is it dead?"

The wise man did not immediately respond. He sat for a few minutes meditating. Then, looking the teenager squarely in the eyes, said, "The answer to that question is completely in your hands!"

Probably, one of the questions that is most frequently asked by those who go into business is, "Will I succeed or will I fail?" Like the fable above, the answer to that question is completely in our hands.